THE FABLES OF AVIANUS

The Tortoise and the Eagle

The Fables of
AVIANUS

Translated by DAVID R. SLAVITT

With a Foreword by Jack Zipes

Illustrations by Neil Welliver

The Johns Hopkins University Press

Baltimore and London

The Johns Hopkins University Press
2715 North Charles Street
Baltimore, Maryland 21218-4319
The Johns Hopkins Press Ltd., London

LIBRARY OF CONGRESS CATALOGING-IN-PUBLICATION DATA
Avianus.
  [Fabulae. English]
  The fables of Avianus / translated by David R.
Slavitt : with a foreword by Jack Zipes : illustrated
by Neil Welliver.
    p. cm.
  ISBN 0-8018-4684-6 (hard : acid-free paper)
  1. Fables, Latin—Translations into English.
2. Animals—Poetry. I. Slavitt, David R.,
1935– . II. Title.
PA6225.E5 1993
873'.01—dc20   93-12828

A catalog record for this book is available from the
British Library.

Fables IX and XXXVI first appeared in David R. Slavitt's *Vital Signs,* Doubleday, 1975.
Fables XVII, XXII, and XLII appeared in *Grand Street,* 1993. Fable XLI appeared in *The
Shenandoah Review,* 1993.

For Stephen Sandy

Contents

Foreword: Avianus Reborn

When the word fable is mentioned one automatically thinks of the name Aesop, never Avianus. Indeed, history has not been very kind to Avianus. Despite the fact that very little is known about the life of Aesop, he is still regarded as the father of the fable, and all sorts of legendary accounts of his life as a wise and cunning slave have been passed on to us from antiquity. By contrast, scholars have not spent much time researching the life of Avianus, though his verse translations of Babrius's fables were extremely popular during the Latin Middle Ages and helped keep the Aesopic tradition alive during this time. The influence of Avianus's fables can be found in schoolbooks and the works of other Latin writers, and it is difficult to tell why their popularity waned. Perhaps it was due to the rise of the vernacular languages and the publication of more interesting fables by such gifted writers as Marie de France, La Fontaine, and Lessing during the seventeenth and eighteenth centuries. Whatever the case may be, Avianus's fables were undeservedly relegated to dusty shelves and were never fully translated into English verse. Now, thanks to the remarkable efforts of David Slavitt, we have the complete forty-two elegiac fables composed by Avianus and an opportunity to reacquaint ourselves with one of the more popular "minor" Latin writers of fables during the medieval period.

Of course it is impossible to discuss Avianus's fables without tracing their connection to the Aesopic tradition. As is well known, Aesop never wrote down his own fables, and they were preserved during the sixth century B.C. only by word of mouth. Given their obvious concern with power and the relations between slave and master, the fables were probably considered somewhat subversive and certainly provocative during his lifetime. When the Greek city-states established freedom of speech shortly after Aesop's death about 560 B.C., rhetoricians began using the fables to teach students rules of grammar and to discuss morals and ethics, because these stories were short and exemplary in their manner of argumentation and resolution.

Many Greek writers were influenced by the Aesopic fables. By 300 B.C. Demetrius Phalerius, a notable Athenian statesman, founded the Alexandria Library and recorded two hundred fables in Greek prose entitled *Assemblies of Aesopic Tales*. These fables soon became the models for Alexandrian scholars and scribes and were circulated throughout the Mediterranean in Greek. Meanwhile, there were other collections of fables from India that also became popular in the region. For instance, the tales of the legendary story-teller Kasyapa formed the corpus of the Libyan fables of "Kybises" and were eventually combined with other well-known fables by a scholar named Nicostratus at the court of Marcus Aurelius. Then, in the first century after Christ's death, Phaedrus, a Greek slave freed by the Emperor Augustus, turned the Greek fables of Phalereus into Latin iambics, and he was followed by Valerius Babrius, tutor to the son of Alexander Severus during the latter part of the first century, who took three hundred of the Aesopic and Libyan fables and developed his own versions in Greek verse with Latin meters.

The collections of Phaedrus and Babrius were well known and played a major role in the development of the fable during the rise of the Roman Empire. Therefore it is not surprising that, toward the end of the fourth century, Avianus, a young Roman poet, decided to transpose forty-two of Babrius's fables into Latin verse. Avianus is described in Macrobius Theodosius's *Saturnalia* as a modest and virtuous youth, who rarely spoke; but when he did, he maintained the conversations through his wry questions and objections. In addition, he tells several delightful stories in the *Saturnalia* and is admired for his wit and memory.

It is not clear when and why Avianus, sometimes spelled Avienus, wrote his fables. Some scholars believe that they were written about A.D. 400, while others have argued for A.D. 430. Avianus seems to have belonged to a coterie of poets who gathered around the gifted Macrobius Theodosius. By translating Babrius's Greek fables into Latin elegiacs, Avianus elevated the stories so that they could be regarded with more respect as *literature* with a moral purpose. His literary ambitions are evident in the manner in which he sought to imitate Ovid and Virgil. In addition, part of his purpose was apparently to preserve interest in the Roman customs and religion, for Avianus was a pagan. The particular kind of Latin usage he cultivated in his poems was close to popular speech. Though Avianus took liberties with the hexameter couplets, and though his linguistic constructions and vocabulary reflect the decline of Latin in the fourth and fifth centuries, his poems were metrically correct and evidently well received. As I have mentioned before, they formed one of the most popular collections of fables during the Middle Ages. In fact, there were numerous translations of his work and prose paraphrases in Europe up through the seventeenth century, and many of his fables were used separately in primers.

Like the stories of his predecessors, Avianus's fables were used to teach the rules of rhetoric and ethics to young students. Given their pagan references and allusions, however, the fables may have played a "subversive" role during the rise of Christianity in the Middle Ages. Not that Avianus was a rebel. If anything, he was more concerned with elevating the Aesopic fable tradition in a poetical form that combined eloquence with humor and ethics. In his dedication to Macrobius Theodosius, he stresses that, aside from Aesop, his models were Socrates and Horace, who used amusing stories as examples for young people to read and follow. In other words, Avianus was very knowledgable about the literary and philosophical tradition of the fable and sought to employ the comic aspect of the genre to make his moral messages even more efficacious than they might have been in a serious prose narrative.

If one were to compare Avianus's fables with those of Babrius, the differences are striking, and it becomes apparent why Avianus became so popular during the Middle Ages. First of all, it is difficult to estimate how well Babrius's fables were known in their Greek original. In fact, the British scholar Alan Cameron has argued that Avianus himself may not have known Greek and may have used a Latin prose translation of Babrius's fables by Julius Titianus as the basis for his Latin verse translation. Whatever the case may be, Babrius's fables are succinct and serious. There are approximately two hundred fables known to have been written by him, and they all are carefully structured and end with some kind of didactic moral or epimythium. Avianus, in contrast, is much more playful and ornate, and he endeavors to incorporate the moral as part of an ironic plot. Though the references to the Roman gods in the fables indicate that Avianus believed somewhat in the Roman religion, they are also satirical and reveal that the gods are not in complete control of the world. For instance, in "The Greedy Man and the Envious Man," Avianus sardonically displays how the gods cannot really mediate between humans who, due to their unpredictable nature, are incapable of benefiting from divine gifts and intervention. In "The Shopkeeper and the Statue," Bacchus lodges a complaint about how his statue is being treated by mere mortals:

"Who in the hell are you
to decide my fate? What kind
of world is this, when a clerk
can determine the life of a god?"
What happened then? Does it matter?
The point is the god's complaint
chastens us all, that the whole world is
contingent on such people's whims.

These lines are Slavitt's very free interpretation of the accusation made by Bacchus and the moral lesson implied by Avianus. But they do reflect Avianus's attitude toward the gods and his criticism of the irresponsibility of humans. Altogether, Avianus's fables show a world in flux, a topsy-turvy world, in which humor and cunning constitute the only saving grace for humans—and, one might add, the poet. One can no longer rely on advice of the old, nor is this advice wise. As can be seen in "The Crab and Its Mother," Avianus's fables construe cynical morals that are often ambiguous in meaning. While remaining true to the Aesopic spirit of depicting scenes of survival of the fittest in a blunt and candid manner, Avianus is fond of hyperbole and the grotesque, and he skillfully employs his hexameters to bring about an ironic twist that makes the reader question traditional assumptions and stereotypes.

Barking dogs, they say,
don't bite—but the other way
is not so straightforward and clear.
Ought we always to fear
a silent spaniel or hound,
avoid it, and give ground?

Writing at a time when the Roman world was being transformed by the rise of Christianity, Avianus appears to voice doubt and skepticism about humankind's capacity to deal with change. But Avianus's voice was not a voice of despair. Again like Aesop, there is a clear preference in his fables for learning how to survive and for the underdog, as can be seen in the wonderful closing lines of "The Oak and the Reed," when the reed (again in Slavitt's free translation) says to the oak:

> "There can be
> safety in weakness.
> See how you were strong, fought the winds, defied them, stood
> tall, and endured their entire awesome strength,
> or tried to, but we were pliable, weak, swayed and gave way,
> agreed with whatever the winds proposed,
> moved this way and that, and, offering almost no resistance,
> baffled its crude might.
> It isn't what you'd call noble, or even particularly admirable, but
> we're still standing, are still here."

Avianus's fables are also still here, not, of course, in any literal sense as relics. Rather, they are here in the splendid translation by David Slavitt, who has transposed the difficult metrics of Avianus into lively English verse and added his own droll humor to Avianus's polite irony. Slavitt has accomplished this feat by altering the rhyme schemes and meter, taking liberties with the original texts, and introducing current slang and allusions. It is because of Slavitt's poetic license that Avianus can now be appreciated as a "contemporary" commentator on the "postmodern condition." There are many parallels that one can draw between Avianus's times and our own, and thanks to the fact that Slavitt has placed his finger on how

old and new world orders collide in his fables, Avianus has been
reborn as a shrewd poet who can still instruct us about hypocrisy
and delight us by overcoming adversity just as well as his savvy
master Aesop.

Jack Zipes

Translator's Preface

My motives in addressing Avianus were, I can now confess, mostly ignoble. To be candid, I had begun to feel a bit oppressed by Virgil, Ovid, and Seneca, or, more specifically, I had found it irksome always to be standing on my tiptoes and trying to excel—which is what their poetry so constantly and so magisterially requires. I had begun to dream of some less demanding, chummier body of work, where that dismal obligation to be better wouldn't apply. I wanted, in short, a poet to whom I could condescend, and to whom my attention—or any attention, for that matter—would be a favor.

And there he was, in the Loeb Classical Library's appealingly unintimidating volume *Minor Latin Poets*, the very fellow, a writer whose name I did not remember ever having heard: Avianus. (Or perhaps Avienus?) The P.D.Q. Bach of Latin poetry! A decadent, bumbling fabulist, whose work I could do with one hand tied behind my back. (And any felicity that I managed to achieve in the work would be credited not to him but to me!) Isn't that what a translator dreams of?

Perhaps so, but dreams are wishes and fears that can lead us to actions in the waking world—in which, inevitably, there is surprise and, sometimes, moral correction. I began playing with Avianus, figuring to do only a suite of some of the easier ones, the sillier or more laughable performances. . . . And, of course, I got hooked. I began to find that there was an elegance, a playfulness, a knowing manipulation of the *faux naif* posturing that was extremely pleasing, and that—I came inevitably to realize—was his! I'd found a poet who was minor perhaps, but excellent! And once again I was trying to be just a little shrewder, a little more graceful, a little more suave than I probably am—not to show off but in order to convey with some plausibility that world-weariness, that charm, that elegant *arrière-garde* fussiness I had grown to admire and now wanted to share with friends and like-minded readers (these are probably not different categories).

But why am I making this confession? The real reason is that I became convinced, after having invested some time and attention on these diversions, that my relation to the work of Avianus was not at all unlike his to the tradition of fables that he had chosen—in perhaps the very same spirit—to play with. These stories, the texts of rhetoricians and grammarians, were not only commonplaces of the culture but had about them that special tang of the schoolroom, the redolence that is a blend of varnish, chalk-dust, and the mysterious greenish powdery substance the janitor keeps in the store room to spread on the floor when some youngster throws up. To start with such tired and bookish lumps of material and to polish them so that they shine as bright as new—brighter than new!— was, I grew to believe, Avianus's motive and delight. There may not have been a word for "camp" in fourth-century Latin, but the Romans were surely able to achieve it, recognize it and enjoy it.

Translation, like reading, is not only an intellectual but a spiritual exercise. Dryden's friend, the Earl of Roscommon, in his "Essay on Translated Verse," suggests this psychological and spiritual aspect of the undertaking:

> Examine how your *Humour* is inclin'd,
> And which the *Ruling Passion* of your Mind;
> Then, seek a *Poet* who *your* way do's bend,
> And chuse an *Author* as you chuse a *Friend*.
> United by this *Sympathetick Bond*,
> You grow *Familiar, Intimate* and *Fond;*
> Your *Thoughts*, your *Words*, your *Stiles*, your *Souls* agree,
> No Longer his *Interpreter*, but *He*.

If this is a grotesque boast to make, it is also a grand ambition to entertain—and a heavy responsibility to bear. I wanted to have some relaxed fun, and I did have fun, but it wasn't relaxing. I was up on my tiptoes once again. But if I have succeeded well enough to suggest to an indulgent and imaginative reader something of my admiration for this minor Latin poet, and if I have brought his work some degree of attention in this iron time, it will have been worth it.

▪ ▪ THE FABLES OF AVIANUS

The Nurse and the Child

The baby was bawling, squalling, throwing a tantrum
as babies will, and the nurse, a country woman,
threatened the child with that old ridiculous threat
country people resort to: "You hush up now
or I'll set you out as a treat for the wolves to gobble,
and see if you won't quieten then." The youngster,
perhaps amused by this picturesque locution,
subsided and at length fell asleep. THE END,
or it is for those two. Nevertheless, outside,
a wolf that was passing by happened to hear
what the nurse had said, and didn't think it was funny
or stranger in any way than what human beings
ordinarily do. He resolved to wait
for the next obstreperous moment, show of temper,
or crying fit . . .
                    and waited, and waited, for weeks.
But nothing happened. The nurse never appeared
with that promised *blanquette de bébé*. He slunk on home
to Mrs. Wolf, beside herself with annoyance
and, even worse, contempt. And the moral is:
that that's how women are—you get taken in
and made a fool of by one, which is bad enough,
but then you have to go home and endure the scorn,
the ridicule of your wife on that account?
It's more than any man should have to bear!

The Tortoise and the Eagle

Slow and steady, yes, you can beat a hare-
brained rabbit once in a while, but look up there
    in the blue sky
    where birds fly,
dip, and soar in effortlessness and song,
while the silent tortoise drags his great bulk along
    slowly in the dust,
    moving, but only just.

One tortoise, his belly full, offers a deal
to an eagle—riches, pearls and gems, if he'll
    give him a ride
    and let him glide
and swoop like that, at breath-taking height and speed.
Baubles and wealth are not what eagles need,
    but the fawning tortoise says, "Please,"
    and the eagle at last agrees.

So up they go, and the tortoise, loving it, screams
in delight: "I'm flying, flying as in my dreams,
    but higher, and faster.
    Oh, I am master
of all I survey. I want it never to stop . . ."
At which point the eagle lets the damned tortoise drop.
    They defeat, on occasion, hares,
    but oughtn't to put on airs.

The Crab and Its Mother

The sidling crab, edgewise, was making its random way
    away from something, possibly even toward
something—it would arrive eventually somewhere—
    and in this process bumped itself on a rock.
His mother, exasperated, chastised his gracelessness:
    "Why can't you look where you're going, go where you're
        looking,
pick up your feet, put your best foot forward, try
    a little harder, stand up straight, pay attention,
put yourself sometimes in the other person's shoes,
    show a little consideration, a little
respect? If I've told you once, I've told you a thousand times!
    It's only for your good I'm saying these things,
so pay attention, wipe that silly smile off your face!
    One fine day you'll realize that what I'm saying
is not unimportant . . ." And so on, and on and on and on.
    When she subsided, or anyway paused for breath,
her obstreperous child replied, "Oh, stop your endless crabbing!"
    There could be a moral lesson in this somewhere.

The Wind and the Sun

So the sun and the wind get to talking—
	shooting the breeze, one might say—
about which of the two is the stronger,
	and one suggests there is a way
to settle the question: a contest.
	Let the powers of each one be tried
by a stranger—that one, for example,
	on the road down there. Let him decide!
"And how do we do that?" the wind asks.
	"Make speeches, and then let him vote?"
"Not at all," the sun answers. "We'll see which
	can force him to take off his coat."
The wind takes a deep inhalation
	and blows out as hard as it can,
but this seems not to have much effect in
	removing the coat from the man.
The other contestant commences,
	and sends down those warm rays that you
bask in on beaches. And quickly,
	the man opens one button, two.
More rays, and more buttons, until he
	takes off the whole garment. The sun
beams, as it were, and announces
	"You see? Now admit it. I've won."
Conceding the loss, the wind moans in
	self-pity—and moans and howls yet,
for his idiocy in agreeing
	to such a ridiculous bet.

The Donkey and the Lion's Skin

A donkey finds, somehow, a lion skin,
and for a lark he gets himself dressed in
    that pelt.
         Why not
have a little taste of what the lion's got,
    that grandeur and that great pride?
Why should he not seek them with this hide?

Sheep bleat in fear, and cows and heifers moo.
No horse will say him nay! A dream come true,
    for who
         would dare
defy that diadem of lion hair?
    They're none of them wholly insane
and do not test the donkey's might or mane.

But after a little time the farmer appears,
who laughs and seizes one of the donkey's ears.
    "You fraud!
         You fake!
Only a fool or stranger could mistake
    you for a lion. In front, you pass;
but from behind, one recognizes: ass."

The Crab and Its Mother

The Frog and the Fox

A frog leapt off her lily pad to rove,
leaving her pond to explore a nearby grove,
where she set herself up in the practice, if you please,
of medicine. Any ailment or disease
she undertook to cure, prescribing waters
to skeptical beasts for themselves and their sons and daughters,
and leeches for their friends to thin and cleanse
the blood. She gave dietary regimens
to the very fat and thin. And patients came
from all through the wood, through which her healer's fame
spread, as Apollo's heir and Paeon's too—
until a vixen asked her, "What can you,
so pale, so green, so oddly shaped, so squat,
know about health? Whatever it is you've got,
I shouldn't wish to catch. Yourself, heal first,
who, of all creatures here, look much the worst.
You a physician? It has to be a joke!
Following your advice, we'd all of us croak."
The vixen laughed—she really was quite bad—
and the frog hopped it, back to her lily pad.

The Vain Dog

Barking dogs, they say,
don't bite—but the other way
is not so straightforward and clear.
Ought we always to fear
a silent spaniel or hound,
avoid it, and give ground?
One such dog there was,
that, without evident cause,
would suddenly snap and bite
whatever offended his sight.
His master, displeased and disgusted,
and knowing it couldn't be trusted,
put a bell on its neck to alert
passersby, who'd be otherwise hurt.
In no way embarrassed or cowed,
the dog was exceedingly proud
of this ornament that he now wore,
which he took to parading before
his pals in the neighborhood—but
one not quite so gullible mutt
laughed at him, asking, "How come
you think the whole world is so dumb?
You can't put us dogs on that way
pretending to be distingué:
we know it's no order of valor
that's dangling down from your collar.
As anyone plainly can tell,
it's a fool's or a leper's bell."

Jupiter and the Camel

You should be content,
whatever your lot,
not worrying that
the next man's got
much more than you,
for it does no good
to fuss and stew.
Better, you should
offer up the thanks
and praise that are due
to the gods above—
as the camel learned,
who so displeased Jove.

The camel's a great shambly ugly beast
and sulky, understandably, for his life
is hard, plodding the desert, carrying Arabs'
huge tents and all those pots and pans,
but his gripe is other, older, and deeper seated.
There used to be camels like him but with huge ears,
long as rabbits' ears or donkeys', but bigger,
that gave the camel a look, not handsome exactly,
but it had, let us say, cachet.
                              It came to pass
that the Lord of Olympus, perhaps on one of his quests
for erotic adventure, found himself and a camel
vis-à-vis, tête-à-tête, and the beast
took advantage of this rare chance and complained
that he wanted horns,

like the antelope has, and the other
various ungulates: antlers, weapons, protection
and not at all bad looking.
                    "It isn't fair,"
he groused to the lord of the sky, "to be unprotected
and vulnerable to predators this way."
Jupiter touched the camel and, voilà!
the gorgeous ears were gone—to teach it a lesson,
not to complain, not to be such a pest.
So all the camel can do nowadays is spit.

The Two Companions and the Bear

The road dark, the country wild, the pair
already terrified, the hungry bear
was more than a mere projection of their mood,
but shaggy with lumbering life and out for blood.
One of the travelers, lucky or quick, ascended
a tree, but the other, alone after what his friend did,
collapsed on the spot, played possum, became a ball
of helpless flesh desiring to be small.
The bear approached and with an inquiring nose
poked at his obstinate bulk, while his blood froze.
It hesitated. No bear wants to eat
carrion, after all. With one of its feet
it prodded the quondam tidbit, and then went off.
From up in the tree, a tactful inquiring cough,
and: "You all right?"
                          The blood thawed and flowed,
and the supine fellow picked himself up from the road.
"A hell of a thing," said the one coming down from the tree.
"It was," said the other. "You know what the bear said to me?"
"It *said?* It spoke? What did it say?"
                                        "To end
my association with you, you no-good-son-of-a-bitch, piss-ant
          bastard excuse for a friend."

The Bald Cavalier

Onto the Champs de Mars, the cavalier
makes his grand entrance. Behold his noble steed
that canters and gallops splendidly. . . . Ah, but we fear
the effect is somewhat diminished by the deed
of the ungallant wind—that takes his rug
and whisks it into the air. The bare-domed rider
hears the guffaws of the crowd and with a shrug
admits the disaster. His grin, as he speaks, grows wider:
"It's quite absurd, I know, and I join in your laughter.
First my hair flees, and now my wig flees after."

The Two Jars

It rained for days, and the river, as rivers do,
overflowed its banks, eroding them here and there,
and on this occasion taking with it two
jars it swept along, an ill-matched pair,
although they both were handsome enough, for one
was of hammered bronze; the other, earthenware.

They seemed in the current to frolic like children at play,
as the clay, and then the metal, bounced ahead.
But the bronze called out a warning, "Keep away!
We mustn't damage each other." The clay pot said,
"It's nice of you to pretend to such concern,
but whichever hits the other, I wind up dead."

The Farmer and the Treasure

Cultivating his field one day, a farmer
feels the blade of his plow encounter . . . a rock?
Or, no, it's a buried box. A coffin? A coffer
of gold, no less! He's dumbfounded, in shock,

but in time it sinks in. His life is changed, not rich,
but comfortable. He can buy a better field,
more stock perhaps, take pride and even comfort,
as a man should be able to do from his labor's yield.

Prudent, he offers his thanks at the goddess's altar,
a token in honor of Earth for her bounteous gift.
Fortuna, however, that night appears before him
in his dream to let him understand she is miffed:

"No incense for me? No flowers upon my altar?
No drop of frankincense? Not even myrrh?
If you'd been a total lout, I shouldn't have minded,
but it's galling to me that you gave thanks to her.

And when you come to grief, your gold's been stolen,
your crops have failed, and your farm's about to go
on the auction block, remember me, Fortuna,
to whom you will pray in your fathomlessness of woe."

The Bull and the Goat

A huge bull charged through underbrush, pell-mell—
one might have thought, if one watched as it sped—
until the mighty lion from which it fled
roared into view, a predator from hell.

The bull, at the limit of its strength, took note
of the mouth of a cave kind gods had provided there,
a sanctuary, fortress, refuge, lair.
He entered—and was confronted by a goat,

cave-dweller, owner, whose bleated baleful bidding
was for him to begone at once. "This cave is fine
for one, and I am he, and it is mine.
No bull!" the goat declared, and wasn't kidding.

The bull smiled and addressed him: "My good man,
if I'm not welcome here, I will not stay.
And if some ravening lion comes this way,
make my excuses to him, as best you can,"

understanding the goat would come to grief
and, by that so fierce feline's rough reproof,
be corrected—to the bull's behoof,
with whom that lion now would have no beef.

The Monkey

Never mind why—the gods behave with whimsy—but once,
    Jove decided to hold a cute-baby contest,
and invited all the world's creatures to enter their kiddies,
    every beast of the earth, and fish of the sea,
and bird of the air. And they came (oh, of course they came!)
    fussing and cooing, their youngsters gussied up
in ribbons and bows. The fish had scales that gleamed like jewels,
    and the little birds with their iridescent plumage
looked like a cunning jeweler's simulacra of birds.
    The mothers paraded their darlings before the god
in a grand procession, and Jupiter nodded, beamed, and preened,
    congratulating them all and of course himself . . .
And then, at the critical moment, just before the awards,
    a mama monkey appeared, pushed herself forward,
and put her wizened wee one down on the floor before him,
    a kind of hairy prune with arms and legs,
and a face that could stop a thousand clocks. And the god laughed!
    And everyone else laughed, and the baby monkey
blinked its pop-eyes, and smiled, and everted its lower lip,
    and everyone roared the louder, until the mother
called them all to order: "Let the god decide
    however he will, and give the prizes out . . .
What does it matter? This is my child, my darling, my love,
    the dearest baby in all the universe."
And again there was laughter, but quickly it gave way to silence
    and awe before her blind passion's truth.

The Crane and the Peacock

You are an altogether dreary bird,
      drab, dull, dun, and totally boring!
   This was the peacock's uncongenial word
      to the plain crane, who seemed to be ignoring
   these jibes and taunts pretty well—until the cock
      lifted his tailfeathers to display
   greens, golds, deep blues, and other hues to mock
      the other's uninterrupted brownish-gray.
   "How can you endure to look like dirt?
      You disgrace all birds and are a sorry thing!"
   the peacock declared. The crane appeared unhurt,
      exerted himself, took wing
   and rose into the air to glide and wheel
      as the peacock could not do. "What sorry kind
   of bird keeps to the ground that way? Big deal
      that you wear that decoration on your behind,
   but it's altogether useless, foolish, dumb,
      and doesn't in the slightest signify.
   Fold it away. It doesn't impress me, chum.
      One hardly even sees it from up in the sky."

The Oak and the Reed

A wind like you've never seen, an unbelievable gale, howled down
from the mountains, in
frenzy, like a live, a malevolent, crazed creature, tearing at roofs,
trees, whatever
had the misfortune to be there in its path, the foolish effrontery to
exist. And among
the victims of this gale there was one lofty, lordly, and venerable
oak tree, torn
huge roots and all from the earth, upended, and flung
unceremoniously into the churning
current of a river that tossed it from bank to bank, that toyed with
it, and then, like a bored child,
or, better, say, a maniac that has turned to other more interesting
victims, let it
come to rest among a growth of reeds, where the still living spirit
of the tree, dazed, faint,
but alert enough, asked, "What sense does this make that I, a
mighty oak, should be uprooted
by the storm, while you delicate and fragile reeds survive,
altogether unharmed?
Explain it to me!" and one of the reeds whispered in reply, "There
can be safety in weakness.
See how you were strong, fought the winds, defied them, stood
tall, and endured their entire awesome strength,
or tried to, but we were pliable, weak, swayed and gave way,
agreed with whatever the winds proposed,

moved this way and that, and, offering almost no resistance,
      baffled its crude might.
It isn't what you'd call noble, or even particularly admirable, but
      we're still standing, are still here."

The Hunter and the Tiger

A hunter there was, a master at it, shrewd
and brave, who went after beasts of any sort.
He came to the wood each day to kill for meat,
for pelts, and also—and not least—for sport.

The animals fled before him, but he persisted,
tracking them down—until they turned in despair
to a tiger whom they feared but asked to help them,
pleading in terror before her in her lair.

Agreeing, she sauntered forth to hunt the hunter
and try her might against his when they found
each other, as they did at last—he flung
his great spear at her flank. She felt its wound,

roared out in pain, and slunk away, the bloody
shaft of the spear dragging along in the dirt.
She crawled into a thicket she knew to rest and
try to draw out of her side that spear that hurt

so dreadfully. As she lay there, a little vixen
approached to ask, "What does he look like? The wood
is eager to know whatever you can remember!"
The tiger moaned, "I remember only my blood."

That's what the hunter you have to fear will look like—
your destiny, your fate, your blood. It's true.
Somewhere out there, even as we are talking,
your death is coming closer. It looks like you.

The Four Oxen and the Lion

Once in a meadow four great oxen stood
together, shoulder to shoulder, buddies, pals
who left the barn each morning together, grazed
side by side, and went home at night together.
They got on famously—all the beasts in the forest
knew they were friends, and respected them for it, for any
fool could see they were safer that way from danger
of predators, say, those hooves, those awesome horns
aligned, making an armed fort of the field.
Even the lions looked at them with awe,
until one, older and sly, approached these beasts
to whisper to the one on the end: "Why you,
on the end that way? It's safer, I'd think, in the middle?
Do you always stand on the outside? Do you trade places?
How does it work? I'm curious to know."
They'd never paid attention before, and the question
was reasonable enough, but the oxen argued,
debated which had risked the outside position,
and which should now stand where to make it fairer,
make up for the past inequities . . .
                              And they quarreled,
and blamed one another for quarreling. Bitter words
were spoken that could not be unsaid, and they each
stood alone the next day, and the next.
And the lion returned to pick off first one, then another,
and then one of the pair that was left. And the last,
as the lion rushed upon it and tore its flesh,

cried out: "Let this be a lesson to all the world
not to give ear to strangers who speak with guile,
or forget old friends . . ."

And then he bellowed and died.

The Pine and the Bramble Bush

It takes a while, but you can hear them sometimes, when the wind
        is right, and picks up their faint voices,
the conversation of plants, the way they can talk to one another,
        clearly enough but so slowly
that you have to stay very still for a long time before you even
        begin to notice that a conversation has been going on.
Thus, these two, a pine tree, tall and graceful, lord of the hillside,
        and, at its base, spreading out somewhat, the way they
        do,
a bramble bush, and they'd been there for years and years, in a
        peaceful and friendly way, plants being, by their nature,
        gentle.
But the bramble bush began to sense a less-than-agreeable
        message from the pine, an even hostile suggestion
that made the fine hairs of the bramble's rootlets recoil, for the
        pine was intimating that it was not just different but
        better,
as much as saying, "Oh, see how tall I am, how lofty, how
        symmetrical, how upwardly sweeping, how grand! What
        must you think,
so low and squatty, so spread out on the ground, so thorny and
        prickly, to have as your neighbor, constant companion,
and, if I may say, comparison, a so much more beautiful example
        of the vegetable kingdom? It must be a source of irritation
        to you,
my architectural elegance in the shadow of which you have to
        spend your every moment,

with no possibility of escape; it must be all but unendurable." And
the pine soughed and sighed in utterly feigned sympathy.
But the bramble bush said in reply—and this took some time to
accomplish— "No, it's not so bad,
for if I can look up and see your loftiness, so can the shipwright in
need of a mast, and the carpenter in search of his perfect
roof beam,
and the axe is already forged and honed that will come to chop
you down and trim your beautiful limbs one by one,
turning you rudely into nude wood, but they will leave me alone,
because what good am I to them?
And on that painful day, you will learn to hate your grace and
height and wish you were low and gnarled and covered
with my thorns."
And then they stopped speaking, and if their conversation took a
long time, their silences were even more exquisitely
extended,
only the occasional exasperated sigh from the pine tree and, in
reply, the pretense on the part of the bramble bush that it
hadn't noticed—
but to hear them not talking to each other, you would have had to
pay very close attention for a very long time.

The Fisherman and the Fish

On the end of his horsehair line, the fisherman caught a fish,
        nothing to make a trophy of or pose with
on the dock with its huge weight displayed on the scale's face—
        in fact it was rather small—but it addressed
the probably startled fisherman, telling him, "Throw me back,
        let me grow up, and catch me when I'm dinner
for a couple of hearty eaters. Now I am hardly worth
        the trouble of cleaning. You'd get no more than a morsel
of what will be a meal! I'll still be here in the lake
        a year from now. Catch me later! For now,
not out of kindness but only self-interest, let me go."
        The fisherman shook his head and told the fish,
"But they say that a bird in hand is worth two in the bush." The
            fish
        asked, "What have birds got to do with it? I'm no bird!"
The fisherman laughed and answered, "You are a poor fish,
        and stupid to expect that I'm such a huge fool."
And he pulled him clear of the water, and cleaned and cooked and
            ate him,
        in only one mouthful, yes . . . but delicious!

The Oak and the Reed

The Nest in the Wheat Field

A meadowlark had made her nest in a field of wheat
down on the ground where the green of the tender stalks touches
the dark brown of the earth. There in the rustling shade
she lived with her chicky-babes as they grew from tiny puffs
of down into fledglings almost ready to take wing.
One day, while their mama was out looking for food to bring back,
the chicky-babes overheard the farmer who said to his wife
as they walked through the field, "I reckon the harvest time has
          come.
I shall have to ask my neighbors to give me a hand with this."
In terror they told their mama what they had heard him say,
and twittered that now they'd have to flee, flee for their lives.
"Pay it no mind," she said. "We've nothing to fear from the
          neighbors."
A few days later the farmer came back, and this time said,
"The time has really come. I shall ask my friends for help."
In terror they told their mama what they had heard him say,
and twittered that now they'd have to flee, flee for their lives.
"Pay it no mind," she said. "We've nothing to fear from the
          friends."
But then, a few days later, the mama observed the farmer
as he sat alone with a whetstone to sharpen the blade of his sickle.
"Now it is time, my dears. He has given up his dreams
of help from neighbors and friends, and comes himself to reap.
Now it will happen. Stretch your little wings and fly."

The Greedy Man and the Envious Man

Who can read the riddle of men's peculiar minds?
   The Olympian gods guessed but never knew the utter
otherness of mortals until great Jove in jest
figured a kind of contest to test the mettle of men,
verify their virtues or expose the extent of their vices.
Apollo would pick a pair to represent the race
of men and grant them a gift—the fulfillment of any fancy,
with only the one proviso, that whatever A might ask for,
and receive as his reward, B should be dealt double.
Phoebus found his pair, made plain this proposition,
and asked what favor the first might choose. Scheming, he chewed
his lip and lowered his eyelids. His wily want was : "Nothing!"
to keep his companion and rival from reaping a double reward.
Enraged at this, the second saw a way to make some mischief
and lower the level of what was already nasty enough:
"What I should like is to lose the sight of one eye," he suggested,
intent on repaying with interest the favor the first had shown him
and cheating in turn the cheater with a sore disability doubled.
Disgusted and angry, Apollo returned to report to the gods
who wept to hear his words about mankind's astonishing
      meanness.

The Shopkeeper and the Statue

In a window of a chic
boutique was a marble figure
of Bacchus to catch the attention
of passersby with taste
and, not incidentally, money.
Into the shop one day,
a couple of customers came,
one a country squire,
looking to buy the figure
to put in the family crypt,
and the other a city father
who thought it might grace a temple
on the street where he lived. To their offers,
delightfully escalating,
the shopkeeper gave his attention
until, from the window behind him,
the statue addressed him, asking:
"Who in the hell are you
to decide my fate? What kind
of world is this, when a clerk
can determine the life of a god?"
What happened then? Does it matter?
The point is, the god's complaint
chastens us all, that the whole world is
contingent on such people's whims.

The Hunter and the Lion

A hunter pursued a lion, or one could say
as easily it worked the other way,
for the lions do not despise the human game.
They got to know each other, and became
familiars, if not friends. In any case,
they found themselves one day in a holy place,
a graveyard, where the tombstones and the steles
depicted battles, hunts, and epic meals,
and there, where they had paused for breath a while,
the hunter noticed a stone that made him smile.
"Look here," he said. "This carving clearly shows
a truth that every man and lion knows—
that men are masters. See how the human stands
erect and holds a sharp spear in his hands,
while the lion lies before him, head bowed low
in sign of that submission you should show
to me." The lion roared a lion's kind
of laugh and answered back, "You're out of your mind.
All that it proves is that one artist thought
men were the stronger, and that the fool who bought
the gravestone was as ignorant as he.
If lions drew or chiseled, you would see
the creature doesn't fawn but is prepared
to leap up, claws extended and teeth bared,
to demonstrate to this pretender why
he's less than even the least of felidae."

The Boy and the Thief

Oh, sad, sad, the poor boy sat by the well, but all was not well,
    no, indeed, for he wept and wailed, albeit attractively, his head
        so sweetly atilt with the tears running slantwise down his downy
            cheeks
that a thief stopped to ask him whatever was the matter,
at which the poor boy only blubbered the more loudly, but
        managed: "Look
down there, in the well, where my rope has broken, and my
        pitcher, my beautiful golden pitcher
is lost. And I am lost. All is lost! Oh, woe, woe! And at that the
        crook
peered down into the well and thought he saw a glint, or, well,
        yes, something . . .
And seeing how the boy was so poor and defenseless, and that
        such chances do not come often,
he took off his coat, laid it carefully on the ground, and climbed
        down the well to retrieve the treasure—
at which point, of course, the youngster grabbed the coat, and ran,
        ran for his life, into the woods,
the quick boy, the clever but no longer quite so poor boy, leaving
        the thief
to repent not of his cupidity but his stupidity and the gullibility by
        which he had come to grief
and wail to the high gods that they'd been right so to punish him,
        an arrant
knave and, worse, a fool—the water, boy, and trick having been so
        transparent.

The Lion and the Goat

A hungry lion looked up at a crag to see
a solitary nanny goat that grazed
on its rocky height and roared: "It seems to me
  not only peculiar, but crazed,
to work so hard for so little, when down here,
there's all this succulent pasturage so near

and easy. Come down to the meadow. Enjoy the thyme
of your life!" But the nanny goat shook her head and said:
"What you suggest makes sense, has reason (and rhyme),
  but I should wind up dead
if I supposed it was only good you mean
to do me—I fear the counsels of the lean."

The Crow and the Urn

A thirsty crow
once spied an urn
in which there was water,
but oh, no,
it was too low,
no matter how he'd crane and turn
and twist and stretch,
he could not reach
the lovely water,
But you learn
sometimes, from need
or even disaster.
The crow was an attentive bird
to the lessons of so stern a master
as the thirst that drove him nearly mad,
tormenting him that way to teach
arcane lessons of engineering—
for after a time it at last occurred
to him that if he could not reach
the water, he might contrive to make it
rise to a level where he could take it
sip by beautiful sip. He flew
and fetched a pebble to drop into
the narrow-necked urn, and again and again,
until the water he wanted rose
to where it was within the crow's
reach. He dipped his beak to drink,
slake his thirst and take his fill.

Thus, if it doesn't defeat or kill
crows or, for that matter, men,
adversity can make them think.
The very obstacle that tries
their souls can also make them wise.

The Farmer and the Ox

A bad ass is one thing, and trouble enough, but an ox
      that won't mind? It's a constant tribulation.
There was a farmer once who had a mean ox like that,
      a lazy creature that hated the ropes, the yoke,
the plow, the whole idea of cultivating a field.
      What can you do with such a beast? He tried
everything he could think of, cut its horns with a knife
      so as not to let the wicked creature gore him;
he worked out a way to get the yoke on the ox's neck
      dropping it down from a perch over its stall;
and he used an extra-long line to put some distance
      between himself and that malign bovine
that otherwise would try to kick him. But there is a meanness
      that improvises, seems to be inspired,
enlisting the neutral world as its own instrument.
      Thus did the wicked beast paw the earth with its hoof,
churning up grit for the wind to blow in the farmer's face,
      mouth, and eyes, to choke, blind, and enrage
the desperate man who admitted at last that goodness and order
      must always give way to evil and entropy.

The Faun's Guest

His road had been long, bad weather was coming on,
and the stranger, groping his way through the mist, cold,
hungry, and maybe lost, encountered a faun
who invited him in to enter his cave. Made bold

by need, he thanked the kind goat-footed creature,
accepted his invitation, and, crouched by the fire,
blew on his hands to warm them. You're happy to meet your
savior, however odd, when your need is dire

enough. "A drink?" the satyr offered. "Bless
you, sir," the traveler said. The faun brought a bottle
of wine. "And something to eat? Some hot soup? Yes?"
the faun asked as he ladled it out from the kettle.

His guest accepted with thanks but could not sip
because it was so hot. He blew on the potage
to cool it some so it would not scald his lip.
At this, the satyr was frightened. "Get out of my cottage,"

he screamed at his guest. "You're a wizard, warlock, or worse,
with magical powers that frighten me to death,"
the simple satyr exclaimed with a country curse.
"You blow either hot or cold with the same breath!"

The Pig and Its Owner

A pig came rooting into its master's wheat field, trampling down with
   its clumsy trotters the tender stalks,
and the gentleman farmer, irked, drew his pretty knife from its
   scabbard and whack! cut off the pig's ear
to teach him a lesson. But this was a stubborn pig and couldn't or
   wouldn't take the hint,
not even after having, so we may say, lent an ear to the owner's
   earnest counsel. No, he was back
in the same field the next week, and the owner, this time really
   annoyed, cursed the obstinate and intractable pig,
drew his knife, and cut off the other ear, figuring that perhaps he
   had not the first time made his point with sufficient
   clarity and force.
But the pig, unpersuaded, was back the very next day, and this
   time, at the end of his patience (just as the pig was out of
   ears),
the farmer ordered that the stupid animal be butchered forthwith.
   But that's only the beginning of our story,
because that night, at supper, the farmer decided, after the first
   couple of courses, that what he'd like
was a nice plate of fried brains with black butter and capers (It's
   really good! You should try it.)
and sent word to the cook—who'd had the same idea and had
   already fried and eaten the brains himself.
What to do? What to do? The cook came out to the dining table,
   bowed low, and announced to the farmer,
"I'm sorry, master, but brains? That pig, if he'd had any, would still
   be alive and well, rooting for acorns out there in the sty!"

The Mouse and the Ox

A mouse made bold in a barn to attack
an ox—he bit as high and hard
as he could, and the ox, annoyed more than angry,
tried to step on the mouse and kill it,
but the impudent rodent retreated into
his tiny hole from which he taunted
the huge creature that pawed and snorted
so helplessly before him: "Size
is nothing at all, can be a burden.
It doesn't matter how big, or strong,
or rich, or even how smart you are,
it's what you do with whatever you've got
and whether it fits the whims of the world."
And the ox bellowed in impotent anger
as the mouse squeaked and squealed in its triumph:
"Ally, ally oxinfree!"

The Drover and His Oxen

His wagon stuck in the mud, the drover got out,
waded around, shouted, waved his hands,
whipped his beasts, and then, when the wagon still
stayed still, stuck in the muck, he prayed to the gods,
especially Hercules, lord of strength, to come
to his and, of course, his struggling oxen's aid.
A voice came down from the sky: "Before you pray,
you ought to get down in the mud and push, help,
and do what you can, yourself, you lazy lout.
Only if that doesn't work, can you try with prayers,
to which, until then, none of us gods will listen."

The Monkey and One Twin

The Goose That Laid Golden Eggs

You'd think that a golden egg
would be a great thing for a goose
miraculously to produce.
But the farmer who had to wait
for each day's small allotment
didn't like seeming to beg.
To wait for what he got meant
the goose was the master, not he.
So it wasn't perhaps so great.
It wasn't real wealth, you see,
but only some comfort and ease,
which isn't sufficient to please
a man with ambitions of scope.
He felt like a perfect dope
going out to that goose each day
to see if she'd deigned to lay.
The slow doling out became
a kind of unpleasant game
or a joke that the gods were playing.
He conceived the idea then of slaying
the goose and thus getting all
that golden hoard at once.
And he did, but nothing was there,
not even a series of small
eggs that the goose might have laid.
He realized at once what a dunce
he had been and filled the air
with wails of self-hatred and woe.

This story is meant to show
that for even slow increase
we should give thankful prayers,
instead of putting on airs
and killing our golden geese.

The Grasshopper and the Ant

Look to the ant, how he toils and labors, bearing his gleanings back
      to the anthill, carrying heavy loads long distances,
      organized, sage,
look to the ant that provides against winter and its hard times,
      against old age, and, taking a page
from his book, learn how to do likewise, think ahead, and
      understand how life
is neither a game, lark, nor bowl of cherries, but a brigand who
      lurks with his long knife,
ready to pounce on any who let down their guard even for a
      moment. O my friend,
consider the ant and his neighbor, the grasshopper who came to so
      sorry an end.
The ant, of course, worked hard all year long, storing up a
      considerable hoard of food,
while the grasshopper sang, enjoying the sunshine and celebrating
      his own and the world's fine mood,
for time past and time future are both abstractions in the minds of
      those who are paying
attention to the gifts of the present, which seem to require as
      thanksgiving our laughing and playing,
to which agreeable enterprise the grasshopper was willing to
      devote himself altogether,
while the ant, otherwise occupied, laid in supplies for the
      inevitable change in the weather—
which all summer long seemed infinitely remote, until, abruptly, it
      happened, and frost

covered the fields, and there was nothing left to eat for the
        grasshopper, who was, alas, lost,
faint with hunger, and cold, cold, cold. "O ant, help me out, give a
        morsel to an old pal! Come on, be a sport,"
the grasshopper pleaded. But the ant replied, "I am not at all
        surprised to see that you are taken short
and that the consequences of your frivolousness are now clear. But
        that I should now help you? Fat chance!
All summer long you sang your silly songs; now, hungry, and
        shivering in the cold, O grasshopper, be a good sport and
        dance!"

The Monkey's Twins

"Oh, God! Good God! Ye Gods!" Grown-ups are always saying
some such thing, not really complaining, but not quite praying
either, and the puzzled boy asks his grandfather what
those gods are like. Could they be grandfathers' grandfathers? "Not
exactly," the grandfather answers, and sits the child on his knee.
"But there is an old fable my grandfather once told me,
and I can tell you, of a monkey who gave birth to twin sons.
As they grew up, the mama monkey decided that one's
smile was a little nicer somehow than that of his brother,
though to anyone else, the one would have seemed much like the
        other.
But that's how it is, sometimes. And there is no good reason why
a parent's heart will melt for one child while the other's cry
produces only annoyance or rage in her. But it can
happen like that, and did, and of course the un-loved one began
to notice the difference, resent it. After a while he became
an unpleasant child. With people I guess it is much the same,
but we can look at those monkeys as gods look down at us
and see how they act, and be pained or perhaps amused at the fuss
they make over nothing, and what strange fixes they get into.
But back to the story. Those monkeys, those little twin brothers,
        grew,
one loved and loving, the other unloved—and nasty, as you
might have expected. But then, a panther, or some such beast,
appeared one day in the forest in search of a monkey feast.
The mother grabbed up her darling and cradled him tight to her
        breast.
The other jumped on her back, and held on to her fur as best

he could, as she ran as fast as the rest of the monkeys away
from the panther pursuing them all. We humans often say
that monkeys are funny, their business silly, and they are fun
in barrels-full, but this was life or death—to run
from a beast that wanted to eat them. As the mother monkey fled
her arms were turning to jelly and her darling into lead.
She felt it slipping, felt him falling, fallen to the ground,
and still she ran, afraid to slow down, look around,
and see what had happened to him. The other, less-favored twin
on her back held on, his arms round her neck under her chin
where his hands were locked together, and he was the one to
      survive,
unloved perhaps, uncared for, but nevertheless alive.
And how do you think the gods looking down through the
      treetops feel
when something like that happens? One of the twins was a meal
for a panther, the other lived and even in time became
the mother's adored son, toward whom she felt the same
special affection she'd had for the one who was lost. It's odd,
but people do things like that. And looking down, a god
scratches his head and asks even greater gods above
what are the limits or use of gods' or of mothers' love?"
"That's a terrible story," the boy exclaims who is able to shrug
whatever's unbearable off. With a grin and a ritual hug
he promises to keep mum to his mom and of course his father,
in exchange for the grandfather's promise tomorrow to tell him
      another.

The Calf and the Ox

S campering the pasture, that's how now,
   the brown cow, a calf still, sees
in the next field, yoked to a heavy plow,
the dumb ox, and stops to shoot the breeze:
"What's that contraption? What kind of life
is that?" The questions, even the mocking laugh
get no rise from the ox, but a silent stare
at the farmer who carries a glittering butcher knife
and a light halter, coming toward the calf.
Nobody gets to choose which yoke to wear.

The Dog and the Lion

Fighting and losing to hunger on the one flank and to fear
        on the other, the old lion came down from the hills
to approach the town with its risks and its easy domestic pickings,
        and there he met a dog, not a watch-dog really
or even a hunting dog, but more of a lap-dog, a pet,
        plump and smug, which is why it addressed the lion
instead of doing what dogs are supposed to do: "Ho, there,
        what a lean lion you are, what a scrawny fellow.
A sad king of the beasts! Or are you a mere pretender?
        Your ribs make an anatomical demonstration!
Where is the grandeur in that? I have my supper dish
        filled every morning and night. As you see, I'm groomed
and combed, my claws are clipped, and my teeth are scraped
        of tartar . . . Look at my coat and my elegant collar.
Mine is a life, while yours is a bare existence, a trial,
        a heavy burden. How on earth do you bear it?"
The lion looked at the dog in surprise and with some annoyance.
        At length he replied: "Collar? And sometimes leash?
Even, at times, a chain, I shouldn't wonder. But I
        can come and go as I please, free to take chances
of a life that is truly my own, while you are somebody's pet.
        All the world's dog-chow piled into a dish
cannot begin to assuage the spirit's essential hungers—
        if you are satisfied, your soul is dead."

The Fish and the Lamprey

A hatchling the current swept down from its spawning ground
found itself at sea, in a world of odd fish,
of whom he was mostly afraid, but he didn't show it.
Instead, he affected disdain for these so bizarre
creatures. What freaks! What weirdnessess they were . . .
A lamprey, one of the petromyzonidae
(which is, you may be assured, an exceedingly ancient
family of fishes), sensing this condescension,
accosted the *auslander* thus: "O Mr. Fish,
you think you are such a splendid catch, so grand,
but you're nothing special. Assume a fisherman's net
in which we are both caught, and imagine a table
where they have us on ice, displayed for sale. My price
is ten times yours—that is, if you're sold at all
and not, at the end of the day, thrown to the cat."
A puzzling story. The lamprey, of course, is correct:
he is a treat. King Henry I of England
is said to have died of a surfeit of lampreys. Still,
a parasite, a plague upon other fish,
he's nothing like Charlie, the Tuna with good taste—
but that is another and equally puzzling story.

The Veteran Burns His Weapons

The old campaigner, out of the service, reaching at last
　　　that home he never expected to see again,
prepared the sacrifice he had promised the gods in times
　　　of danger, discomfort, or most of the time the boredom
of army life—an enormous bonfire onto which
　　　he prepared to throw the weapons he'd brought back,
his own of course, but also those he had taken in battle
　　　or just picked up from abruptly pacific corpses.
One of these souvenirs was a somewhat battered trumpet
　　　which, as he picked it up, blared out in protest:
"Why me? I never did anyone any harm!
　　　I'm a musical instrument, not a weapon."
The veteran shook his head and smashed the horn to the ground,
　　　kicked it against the wall, and then declared:
"At no risk to yourself, you called the others to do
　　　that dirty work you could never manage yourself.
More cruel, and a damnable coward too!" and he threw it
　　　onto the pyre to writhe and melt in remorse.

The Leopard and the Fox

O oh, la la! The leopard preens,
glides along, sashays, parades
its grand rosettes. No jungle scene's
so grand as when a leopard's there,
with its gorgeous pelt and that debonaire
bon ton. "The lion's beauty fades,

to a tawny insignificance
in comparison," the beast maintains,
so pleased with himself. But then, by chance,
a fox pops up to say, "Come, come,
you're handsome enough. But dumb, dumb, dumb!
What are good looks compared with brains?"

The Storm and the Jar

A potter took a vessel from his wheel and set it out
  to dry a while in his garden, the better to take a glaze
  when he fired the piece to finish it—this was the way he worked.
  But a sudden storm came up with rain that fell in torrents.
  Nothing odd, so far, but the rain cloud is reported
  to have noticed the not-yet-fired piece and then to have asked it:
  "Who are you?"
                     At which point the pot is said to have
            answered:
  "I am a jar, an amphora, an *objet d'art!* I am
  that well-wrought urn the poet speaks of; I am a made
  thing, an artifact, a triumph of civilization."
  Which might have been true in the fullness of time, or might not
            have been,
  but surely wasn't yet the indisputable case.
  And the wind, hearing this, howled, we may say, with derisive
            laughter,
  and rain came down on the clay, as if the force of the storm
  were reproving the grand boast and saying, "You're nothing but
            dirt,
  were, are, and always will be. Your name is mud."

The Wolf and the Kid

The kid ran for his very life, cut back,
darted, bolted, wheeled, with a hungry wolf
hot at his heels, the sound of its stertorous breath
roaring in the ears of the terrified goat,
who hardly noticed the huts he'd passed, the barns,
the farmers' houses . . . But then the village walls
were there before him, the gates ajar, and he sped
past and through, and onto the thoroughfare,
where he paused to catch his breath. Against all odds,
the wolf came into the town as well, and sauntered
as bold as brass up that same street to say,
"Look there, one temple after another, and each
with its altar where the victims groan their last and spill
their life's blood, cattle, chicken, sheep—and goats!
You think you are safe here, kid, but think again,
and come back out to the woods and meadows with me.
Out there we can resume our game of tag
where your chances are better than here." The kid replied,
"You've got to be kidding? I'll stay here in the village.
Death is everywhere; no one avoids it. But some
get to choose. Why not elect a noble
end—on an altar with garlands around my neck
and hymns to the gods—instead of a brutal, sordid
demise in which teeth like yours rip at my throat?"
The wolf smiled, saluted, and went on his way.